AMERICAN CARS

THROUGH THE DECADES

American Cars
of the 1980s

Craig Cheetham

GARETH**STEVENS**
GS PUBLISHING
A Member of the WRC Media Family of Companies

Please visit our web site at: **www.garethstevens.com**
For a free color catalog describing Gareth Stevens Publishing's
list of high-quality books and multimedia programs,
call 1-800-542-2595 (USA) or 1-800-387-3178 (Canada).
Gareth Stevens Publishing's fax: (414) 332-3567.

Library of Congress Cataloging-in-Publication Data

Cheetham, Craig.
    American cars of the 1980s / Craig Cheetham.
       p. cm. — (American cars through the decades)
    Includes bibliographical references and index.
    ISBN-13: 978-0-8368-7727-4 (lib. bdg.)
    1. Automobiles—United States—History. I. Title.
TL23.C443 2007
629.2220973′09048—dc22   2006051061

This North American edition first published in 2007 by
Gareth Stevens Publishing
A Member of the WRC Media Family of Companies
330 West Olive Street, Suite 100
Milwaukee, WI 53212 USA

Copyright © 2007 Amber Books Ltd

Produced by Amber Books Ltd., Bradley's Close,
74–77 White Lion Street, London N1 9PF, U.K.

Project Editor: Michael Spilling
Design: Joe Conneally

Gareth Stevens managing editor: Valerie J. Weber
Gareth Stevens editor: Alan Wachtel
Gareth Stevens art direction: Tammy West
Gareth Stevens cover design: Dave Kowalski
Gareth Stevens production: Jessica Yanke and Robert Kraus

Illustrations and photographs copyright International Masters
Publishers AB/Aerospace–Art-Tech

Printed in the United States of America

1 2 3 4 5 6 7 8 9 10 10 09 08 07 06

Table of Contents

Cadillac Allanté

The Cadillac Allanté combined Italian design and American engineering to make a truly international car.

The Allanté's sharp lines were designed in Italy.

The Allanté was a big car, but it was only a two-seater.

Even the earliest Allantés were fitted with **antilock brakes**.

Later versions of the Allante were more luxurious and better built than the earlier cars.

The Allanté **convertible** did not have a power top. The car's top had to be raised and lowered by hand.

The Allanté's square-shaped nose is similar to many European cars of the time.

Cadillac wanted to change its image, so it teamed up with Italian design company Pininfarina. The result was the 1987 Allanté — a car made to compete with top European car makers such as Mercedes and Porsche.

The Allanté's styling was sharp and attractive, but the car was expensive. Allantés were built partly in Italy and partly in the United States. The parts built in Italy were flown to the U.S. in a Boeing 747 jumbo jet. Cadillac workers then fitted the car's engines and interiors.

The Allanté did not sell as well as Cadillac hoped it would because of its high price. The company stopped producing it after just six years.

UNDER THE SKIN

The Allanté's inner body was the same as the Cadillac Eldorado and Seville models.

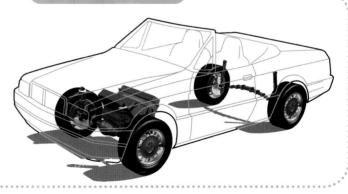

Chevrolet Camaro IROC Z28

The IROC Z28 was the fastest and most desirable of the Camaros built in the 1980s.

The Camaro had a smaller version of the Corvette's V-8 engine.

The Camaro had four seats and a big trunk, which made it very good for carrying people and things, even though it was a **sports car**.

The IROC Z28's wide body and **side skirts** made it easy to recognize.

Camaros were all **luxury** cars. The IROC Z28 had leather seats.

The IROC Z28 had 16-inch (40.6-centimeter) wheels that were used only on IROC Z28s.

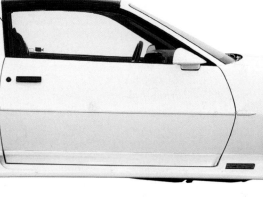

From this angle, the Z28's shape makes it look like a powerful muscle car.

1982

Chevrolet launches the third-generation Camaro, replacing the second-generation model Z28 (pictured below).

1985

The company launches the IROC Z28 version of the Camaro. It is an instant hit with Camaro fans.

The Camaro was one of the best-loved sports cars in the United States, and it always sold well. When a new version was introduced, Chevrolet had to get it right first time.

New Camaro

Launched in 1982, the third generation Camaro was so successful that it kept selling for more than ten years. The squared-off shape was popular with American sports-car fans, while its leather interior was also attractive.

The first Z28 launched in 1982 was fast, but the IROC Z28 was based on Chevrolet's Daytona racers and was even faster. It reached a speed of 160 miles (257 km) per hour.

UNDER THE SKIN

The Camaro IROC Z28 had a simple **suspension** that was made to deal with rough roads at high speeds.

Chevrolet Corvette
Collector Edition

To mark the end of the third-generation Corvette, Chevrolet built a special model called the Collector Edition in 1982.

The 1982 Corvette's rear window lifted up to increase space for baggage.

The car's front end was different from earlier Corvettes. It had a smoother nose and bigger lights.

The Collector Edition had a **T-top** roof with removable glass panels.

Unlike earlier Corvettes, the Collector Edition used **fuel injection**.

The car had multispoke hubcaps.

With its fuel-injected engine, the Corvette was able to reach 60 miles (96 km) per hour in 8.0 seconds.

1980

The Corvette gets a smoother, lightweight body for the 1980s.

1982

Chevrolet launches the Collector Edition, before an all-new Corvette design is introduced in 1984.

The third-generation Corvette had been in production for more than thirteen years. In 1982, before introducing the new fourth-generation Corvette, Chevrolet released the Collector Edition for the car's most dedicated fans.

wheel and side artwork marked it as different from ordinary Corvettes. Chevrolet built only 6,759 Collector Editions. It is rare today.

Luxury Model

The Collector Edition had a silver paint job; a special automatic **transmission**; a leather-trimmed cabin; a special steering wheel; and some minor styling changes, including a new front end. Its special

UNDER THE SKIN

The steel **chassis** under the Corvette's **fiberglass** panels is extremely strong.

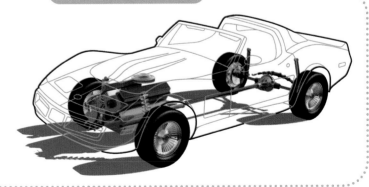

9

Chevrolet Monte Carlo SS Aerocoupe

The Chevrolet Monte Carlo SS Aerocoupe was a sportier version of the company's Monte Carlo.

The Monte Carlo SS's plastic nose was more **aerodynamic** than the nose on standard Monte Carlos.

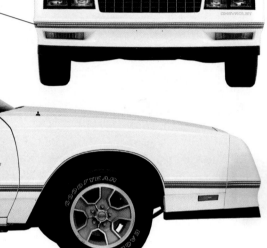

The Monte Carlo looked like it had dual **exhaust pipes**, but it had only one with two holes at the end.

The car's T-top with removable roof panels let in fresh air.

Not much could be fitted into the car's trunk because its mouth was small.

Out on the highway, the Monte Carlo SS Aerocoupe handled smoothly, making it a relaxing car to drive.

1978

The lightweight, economical Monte Carlo goes on sale for the first time.

1986

Chevrolet releases the Aerocoupe to compete with the Ford Thunderbird on NASCAR tracks. The company builds only 6,000 of them.

Throughout the 1980s, the Monte Carlo was Chevrolet's most successful car in **NASCAR** racing. To celebrate its success, the company launched a special model with many NASCAR features.

Extra Features

The Monte Carlo SS Aerocoupe had a huge rear window that made it more aerodynamic. A big 305-cubic-inch (4,998-cc) V-8 engine powered the Aerocoupe. To make it look different from ordinary Monte Carlos, the car had black vinyl trim inside and specially shaped, padded sports seats. The biggest change was at the front, which Chevrolet fitted with a **streamlined** plastic nose.

UNDER THE SKIN

The Monte Carlo has a simple suspension.

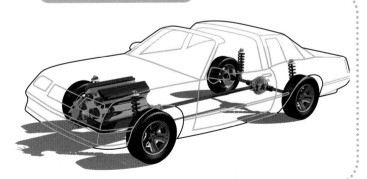

11

De Lorean DMC12

The De Lorean DMC12 was used in the three Back to the Future
movies, which starred Michael J. Fox.

The DMC12's doors
opened upward like
a bird's wings.

The car's engine was
mounted in its back.

All De Loreans
were made
from brushed
stainless steel.
The car's silver
body was
unpainted.

Drivers could open
small sections of the
windows to let in air.

The DMC12 had
a low front end
that made the car
aerodynamic.

Behind the wheel of this DMC12 sits the car's designer, John Z. De Lorean.

1979

John Z. De Lorean gets money from the British government to set up his car company. The first De Lorean car appears in 1981.

1985

Three years after production of the DMC12 stopped, the car is used in the movie *Back to the Future* and becomes famous.

John De Lorean, a former Pontiac design chief, designed the DMC12. It was certainly different from most other cars. Britain's government gave money to De Lorean's company to help develop the car, so a lot of the design and building work took place in Britain.

New Style

The car was, however, designed for the American market. The DMC12 was supposed to compete against cars such as the Chevrolet Camaro and the Pontiac Fiero. People definitely noticed the DMC12's unusual styling, especially its unpainted stainless steel body. The car did not sell well, however, and after two years the car was no longer made.

UNDER THE SKIN

British sports car maker Lotus designed the DMC12's chassis.

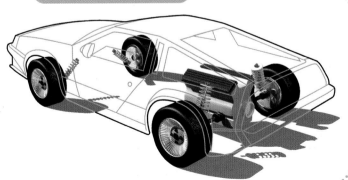

13

Dodge Dakota Shelby

With Carroll Shelby's help, Dodge created a pickup truck with sports-car performance.

The Dakota's simple shape looked modern. It was still built well into the 1990s.

Dakota Shelbys had a strong suspension to keep them from leaning when going around corners, the way many trucks do.

Special Shelby side graphics told buyers that the Dakota Shelby was not the usual Dodge Dakota.

The Dakota Shelby's special Goodyear Eagle GT-4 tires helped it to grip the road.

The Shelby Dakota can accelerate from 0 to 60 miles (96 km) per hour in 8.5 seconds.

1986

Dodge unveils its Dakota pickup truck.

1989

The company announces the Dakota Shelby model. It is available through 100 specially selected dealers.

Today, pickup trucks are very popular in the United States. The best-selling pickups sell better each year than the best-selling cars. The Dodge Dakota began this trend in the late 1980s. The Dakota pickup had a cabin like a car's, gripped the road well, and could go fast. It was the first of its kind.

Call on Carroll

To prove just how good the Dakota was, Dodge asked Carroll Shelby to **tune** 1,500 of them every year. He replaced the truck's 3.9-liter (243-cubic-inch) V-6 engine with a 5.2-liter (318-cubic-inch) V-8 that could put out 175 **horsepower**. The Dakota Shelby could **accelerate** fast, which made it very popular among drivers who wanted a truck with speed.

UNDER THE SKIN

Shelby added a stiff rear suspension and solid **shock absorbers** to the Dakota, which made riding in the Dakota Shelby bumpy.

Dodge Omni Shelby GLH-S

The small hatchback Omni was not a choice for drivers who wanted a fast car until Carroll Shelby turned his attention to it.

The Omni Shelby had black bumpers and driving lights.

The Omni Shelby's taillights had smoked-glass turn signals that were different from those on other Omnis.

The car was available in red or black.

The car's solid tires and special 15-inch (38-cm) wheels appeared only on the Omni Shelby models.

The first Dodge Omnis were inexpensive hatchbacks. With the GLH-S model, an Omni became a great performer.

1978

Dodge introduces the Omni as a rival to the Volkswagen Rabbit.

1986

The company produces a limited run of 500 GLH-S models (pictured below), with an engine that put out 175 horsepower.

The new Omni GLH-S was so fast it could travel at speeds beyond the maximum limit shown on the car's **speedometer**.

The Dodge Omni was designed as a cheap **hatchback**, so few people imagined it could be made into a high-performance car.

Shelby Tuned

Dodge asked the famous tuner Carroll Shelby to turn the ordinary Omni into something special. He improved the Omni's speed by fitting a **turbocharger** to the car's 1.7-liter (125-cubic-inch) engine. The manufacturers also added stiff springs and improved brakes to help the Omni cope with the engine's power.

UNDER THE SKIN

The Omni was based on the French Talbot Horizon.

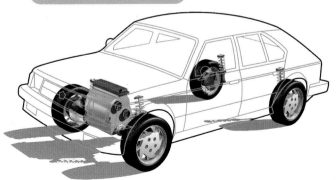

Dodge Shadow Shelby CSX

Tuner Carroll Shelby turned the Dodge Shadow into a high-performance car — the CSX.

The CSX looks like an ordinary Dodge Shadow, a plain two-door budget sedan.

Cool touches on the CSX included a rear wing.

All CSXs had two-tone paint in black over silver, with special Shelby side logos.

The turbocharger, which pumped extra air into the engine, gave the car extra power.

To make the CSX, the body of a regular Dodge Shadow was put on a lower suspension. The lower suspension reduced **wind resistance**, helping the car to go faster.

1987

Dodge's owner, Chrysler Corp, asks Carroll Shelby (pictured below) to help improve the Dodge Shadow.

1989

A limited edition of 500 CSXs appears. The car is so successful that Dodge makes more the following year.

The Dodge Shadow was not an exciting car. Carroll Shelby, who was famous for tuning cars such as the Shelby Cobra and the Mustang GT500, turned the Dodge Shadow from a humble front-wheel drive sedan into a high-performance street machine.

Turbocharged

The turbocharger added by Shelby boosted the engine from 105 to 175 horsepower, giving the CSX a top speed of more than 130 miles (209 km) per hour. Shelby also gave the CSX more powerful brakes and a stronger suspension. Many people thought the CSX was a high-performance car that was surprisingly cheap.

UNDER THE SKIN

The CSX had **front-wheel drive, so most** of the car's weight was at its front.

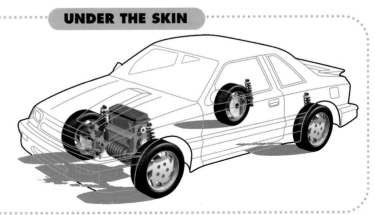

Ford Mustang LX

During the 1970s, Mustangs became a little boring. In the 1980s, the Ford Mustang LX made them interesting again.

The LX had a rear suspension called Quadra-shock that gave the car a smoother ride.

The Mustang LX had simple seating and a practical dashboard.

In 1987, Mustangs were made with rounder edges and a curved front end.

The Mustang LX featured the big, powerful V-8 engine.

The Mustang LX was so quick that police officers across the United States used them as unmarked highway-patrol cars.

1984

Ford introduces the 5.0-liter (305-ci) Mustang LX into its model line (below).

1987

The Mustang LX is redesigned with a rounder front end and bigger headlights.

Ever since the Mustang Mk 2 replaced the original Mustang in the early 1970s, fans were upset that the car had lost some of its power and speed.

New Model

In 1984, Ford brought out the Mustang LX, a model that had a big V-8 engine like the old Mustangs and the performance that Mustang fans had been missing.

Later Mustangs, such as the LX model shown here, put out 225 horsepower — enough power to accelerate from 0 to 60 miles (96 km) per hour in about six seconds. Its fast acceleration made the Mustang LX a true sports car.

UNDER THE SKIN

All the 5.0-liter (305-cubic-inch) Mustang LXs had rear-wheel drive, which gave them extra speed and power.

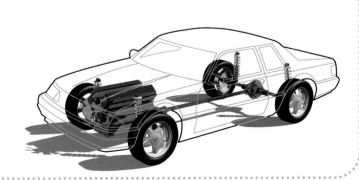

Ford Thunderbird Turbo Coupe

*Ford's first four-**cylinder** Thunderbird was very fast.*

The car's wheels were 16 inches (40.6 cm) wide and came in polished or flat silver.

Early versions of the car had a manual transmission. Later, an automatic transmission was an option.

Fat Goodyear tires gave the car excellent grip on curves.

Later versions of the Thunderbird Turbo **Coupe**, such as the one shown here, had "aero styling" — softer front and rear ends that absorbed some shock if the car crashed.

The Thunderbird Turbo Coupe performed as well as its European rivals, but it was much cheaper and also more reliable.

1982

Ford releases its new smaller, more stylish Thunderbird.

1987

The Thunderbird gets a rounder look, with a new nose and large taillights.

Ford struggled to sell Thunderbirds throughout the 1970s and early 1980s. The company thought that the redesigned 1982 model was the car's last chance for success.

Turbocharged

The new model was very different from earlier Thunderbirds, thanks to a wider choice of engines. Ford buyers were used to models with V-8 engines, but the 1980s Thunderbird had a four-cylinder engine with a turbocharger. This engine made the Thunderbird a very quick car, and it became the top model in Ford's line. Ford had first used this engine, which was designed in Europe, in a limited edition Mustang SVO. The engine used in the 1980s Thunderbird put out 190 horsepower.

UNDER THE SKIN

The Thunderbird had disc brakes all around. These brakes were effective in slowing down the car at high speeds.

Jeep CJ-7

The CJ-7 was a tough car. It was also fun to drive and cheap.

The CJ-7 shown here is the Renegade model. It had a canvas top and a tire cover.

The CJ-7's tall rollbar helped to protect the passengers if the Jeep rolled over.

The plastic lips on the wheel arches were made to cover wider tires.

Drivers used a small lever next to the gear shift to put the Jeep into **four-wheel drive**.

The CJ-7 was a 1980s model, but it looked like the original Jeeps of the 1940s.

The frame, body shape, and basic design of the Jeep CJ-7 are like those of the Jeeps used during World War II.

1984

The 2.5-liter (153-cubic-inch) Jeep CJ-7 appears for the first time.

1988

Jeep introduces the Wrangler to replace the CJ models.

Jeep is one of the most famous American brands. The name "Jeep" comes from the sound of the letters *G* and *P* spoken very fast. "GP" stands for "General Purpose," a phrase the U.S. Army used during World War II to describe these small cars that could drive on almost any surface.

The Jeep's basic design did not change much, even when the Wrangler replaced the CJ-7 in the company's line.

A Popular Car

In the TV show *The Dukes of Hazzard*, Daisy Duke drove the CJ-7. This may explain some of its popularity during the 1980s. The CJ-7 was very cheap and fun to drive — and it always performed better than its rivals.

UNDER THE SKIN

All CJ-7s had a six-cylinder engine that was powerful enough to pull the Jeep up all but the steepest hills.

Pontiac Fiero

With the Fiero, Pontiac offered something new to car buyers.

The engine was hidden beneath a cover in the car's middle.

The version of the Fiero shown here was called the Formula.

When the headlights were switched on, they popped up out of the car's nose.

The Fiero's frame was made out of steel, but its body panels were made out of plastic.

Air **vents** in front of the back wheels gave the engine extra air for cooling.

The Fiero was one of the smallest sports cars on sale in North America. Its interesting design made it stand out from the crowd.

MILESTONES

1983

Pontiac begins production of the Fiero in Detroit, Michigan.

1986

The Fiero is redesigned with a smoother nose and a less wedge-shaped profile.

After years of making big V-8 sports cars, Pontiac decided to try something new — the small Fiero, which appeared in 1983. The Fiero had a small, smooth body. It was designed to compete with small, light Japanese sports cars such as the Toyota MR2.

Mid-mounted Engine

The Fiero's engine was mounted in the center of the car, behind the rear window and in front of the back axle, instead of under the hood. The Fiero's power came from a small 2.8-liter (171-cubic-inch) V-6 engine. Unusually, the car's storage space was under its hood. The Fiero was light, fast, and fun to drive.

UNDER THE SKIN

The Fiero had sports-car looks, but its simple suspension was based on other cars, such as the Pontiac Ventura, the Chevrolet Citation sedan, and the Chevrolet Chevette.

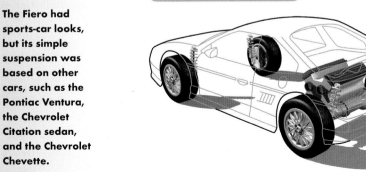

Pontiac Turbo Trans Am

With its turbocharged V-6 engine, the Pontiac Turbo Trans Am was the fastest Pontiac of the 1980s.

Most of the 1,555 Turbo Trans Ams had a T-top roof.

The Turbo Trans Am had front and rear bumpers that were larger and deeper than those on other Trans Ams.

The Turbo Trans Am had gold multispoke hubcaps.

The Turbo had a special suspension system that made it easier to drive at fast speeds.

Inside, the car had electronically controlled leather seats that could be lowered and raised with the push of a button.

MBT 546

The Turbo Trans Am was driven in the Indianapolis 500 race in 1989.

1982

Pontiac introduces its new wedge-shaped Firebird Trans Am (pictured below), which remains on sale until 1993.

1989

To celebrate the Trans Am's twentieth anniversary, Pontiac builds a limited number of Turbo Trans Ams.

For 1989, Pontiac created a special version of the Trans Am to celebrate twenty years of success. This Trans Am had a Buick V-6 engine with a turbocharger, white paint with gold details, and a tan-colored leather interior. It was called the Turbo Trans Am.

Fast Car

The Turbo Trans Am was extremely fast, with a top speed of 157 miles (252.6 km) per hour, making it the fastest Trans Am of all time. The American Sunroof Corporation turned a small number of Turbo Trans Ams into full convertibles. These are the most collectible Trans Ams today.

UNDER THE SKIN

The Turbo Trans Am used the same suspension and steering as a normal Trans Am.

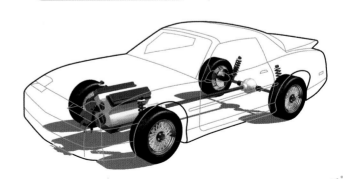

Glossary

accelerate to increase speed

aerodynamic having smooth, sleek surfaces around which air flows easily

antilock brakes brakes that use electronics to prevent a vehicle's wheels from locking

chassis the part of a car body to which the engine, transmission, and suspension are attached

convertible a car with a top that can be lowered

coupe a two-door car, usually seating only two people

cylinder a space inside the engine where a piston is forced up and down by burning petrol to create power

disc brakes brakes that work by pressing a metal plate against rubber pads to slow the car down

exhaust pipes metal tubes that take the gasses resulting from burned fuel away from an engine and make it quieter

fiberglass a lightweight material made from glass strands and plastic

four-wheel drive a system that uses the engine to drive the front wheels and the rear wheels, which gives more grip

front-wheel drive a system that feeds the car's power from the engine to the front wheels

fuel injection used in most modern engines, this system sprays the fuel directly into the engine, improving power

hatchback a car with a door on the rear instead of a trunk, which opens into a storage area

horsepower a unit of measure of an engine's power

luxury special and expensive

NASCAR National Association for Stock Car Racing

rear-wheel drive a system that feeds the engine's power to the wheels at the back of the car

shock absorbers devices fitted to a car that give it a smoother ride on bumpy surfaces

side skirts body panels along the bottom of the sides of the car that give the car a lower look

speedometer a device that measures a vehicle's speed

sports car a car with fast performance and stylish looks

streamlined designed to allow air (or fluid) to flow over a surface smoothly and easily

suspension a system of springs at the base of a car's body that keeps a vehicle even on bumpy surfaces

transmission the system in a vehicle that controls its gears, sending power from the engine to the wheels to make them move

T-top a car roof with a bar down the middle separating two removable glas panels

tuner a person who adjusts cars to make them drive faster and steer and stop better

turbocharger a high-speed fan that forces extra air into an engine to give it more power

V-8 describes an engine that has eight cylinders placed opposite each other in a V-shape

vents slits or openings that take in or let out air or fumes

wind resistance the slowing of a object moving through air as a result of the force of the wind

For More Information

Books

Big Book of Cars. (DK Publishing)

Car. DK Eyewitness (series). Richard Sutton and
    Elizabeth Baquedano (DK Children)

Cars. All About (series). Peter Harrison (Southwater)

Corvette. Hot Cars (series). Lee Stacey
    (Rourke Publishing)

Speed! – Cars. Speed! (series). Jenifer Corr Morse
    (Blackbirch Press)

The Story of the Ford Mustang. Classic Cars (series).
    Jim Mezzanotte (Gareth Stevens Publishing)

The Story of the Jeep. Classic Cars (series).
    Jim Mezzanotte (Gareth Stevens Publishing)

Web Sites

All Muscle Cars
www.allmusclecars.com

Greatest Engineering Achievements of the 20th Century
    — Automobile
www.greatachievements.org

Museum of Automobile History
www.themuseumofautomobilehistory.com

Publishers note to educators and parents:
Our editors have carefully reviewed these Web sites to
ensure that they are suitable for children. Many Web
sites change frequently, however, and we cannot guarantee
that a site's future contents will continue to meet our high
standards of quality and educational value. Be advised
that children should be closely supervised whenever they
access the Internet.

Index